90-Day Gratitude & Reflection Journal

Cheri Perry

Copyright © 2023
Cheri Perry

Performance Publishing
McKinney, TX

All Worldwide Rights Reserved.
All rights reserved. No part of this publication may be reproduced, stored in a retrieval system or transmitted, in any form or by any means, electronic, mechanical, recorded, photocopied, or otherwise, without the prior written permission of the copyright owner, except by a reviewer who may quote brief passages in a review.

ISBN: 978-1-961781-21-4

Be The Sunshine!

This Journal Is a SPECIAL gift for:

From: _____

Date: _____

YOU are my Sunshine!

YOUR GRATITUDE JOURNAL

Be The Sunshine!

Our world needs your **LIGHT!**
Having a daily practice of **GRATITUDE** and **REFLECTION**
will keep that internal light shining- **ENJOY!**

Be The Sunshine!

Mr. Zig Ziglar said that the greatest attitude you can have is the **Attitude of Gratitude!** Cultivating that attitude takes daily, intentional practice AND a fun tool!

Your **BE THE SUNSHINE** Journal is designed to help remind you of all the blessings you have in your life. As you complete each section, you will be reminded of these gifts.
The following pages will explain each section and prepare you for the next 90 days of gratitude and reflection!

When you look for the sun, you find it!

Be The Sunshine!

**You can use this journal any way you like.
Here are a few suggestions for each section.**

RELATIONSHIPS I NEED TO CULTIVATE: Begin by thinking about the friends and family you may want to connect with today.

TODAY I AM GRATEFUL FOR: Then, begin thinking about the things you are grateful for and jot them down.

We usually get what we FOCUS on—which is why the INTENTION part of your journal is so important!

MY INTENTION & COMMITMENT FOR THE DAY: Select a maximum of 2 MAIN areas in your life to focus on today. Write down specific action steps you can take today to fulfill your intentions.

THOUGHTS/BRILLIANT IDEAS/MUSINGS: Use this section to doodle, write down ideas and journal any thoughts or ideas.

REVISIT MY WINS: It's easy to run past our wins so this section gives you valuable reflection time!

WHAT DID I LEARN TODAY: Thinking about adjustments you might have made will give you an opportunity to level up tomorrow.

GOOD NIGHT THOUGHTS/PRAYERS: Ending with a prayer and gratitude will help you sleep soundly with a sense of accomplishment.

QUICK DAILY RATING: Have FUN and pick your SMILEY!

Gratitude & Reflection
turn up the SUN LIGHT!

Be The Sunshine!

Rate each area on your wheel by scoring between 1 and 10. 1 being very poor and 10 being outstanding. Because some life circumstances are beyond your control, choose your score based on 'as much as it depends on me.' Add up each column and divide the total by 10. Take your scores and plot them on the blank wheel on the next page.

Physical
__ appearance
__ regular checkup
__ energy level
__ muscles toned
__ regular fitness program
__ weight control
__ diet & nutrition
__ stress control
__ endurance & strength
__ adequate sleep

__ TOTAL ÷ 10 =

Spiritual
__ believe in God
__ inner peace
__ influence on others
__ spouse relationship
__ church involvement
__ sense of purpose
__ attitude for giving donations
__ prayer
__ Bible study
__ daily devotional

__ TOTAL ÷ 10 =

Financial
__ proper priority
__ personal budget
__ impulse purchases
__ earnings
__ living within income
__ charge accounts kept current
__ adequate insurance
__ investments
__ financial statement
__ savings

__ TOTAL ÷ 10 =

Personal
__ recreation
__ exercise
__ friendships
__ community activities
__ service clubs
__ quiet time
__ growth time
__ consistent life
__ gratitude/reflection
__ building the self-esteem of others

__ TOTAL ÷ 10 =

Be the SUNSHINE
in someone's cloudy day!

Be The Sunshine!

Mental
___ attitude
___ intelligence
___ formal education
___ continuing education & trng
___ creative imagination
___ inspirational reading
___ audible/podcast learning
___ inquisitive mind
___ self-image
___ enthusiasm

___ TOTAL ÷ 10 =

Family
___ listening
___ good role model
___ principled but flexible
___ forgiving attitude
___ build self-esteem of family
___ express love and respect
___ meals together
___ family relationships
___ dealing with disagreements
___ time together

___ TOTAL ÷ 10 =

Career
___ like what I do
___ understand my job
___ co-worker relationships
___ productivity
___ understand biz goals
___ activity/goals relationship
___ appreciate company benefits
___ opportunity for advancement
___ career development
___ well-trained for my job

___ TOTAL ÷ 10 =

CHART YOUR SCORES ➡

Be the SUNSHINE in someone's cloudy day!

TODAY I WILL BE THE SUNSHINE!

DATE:
Let's visualize our current wheel of life assessment!

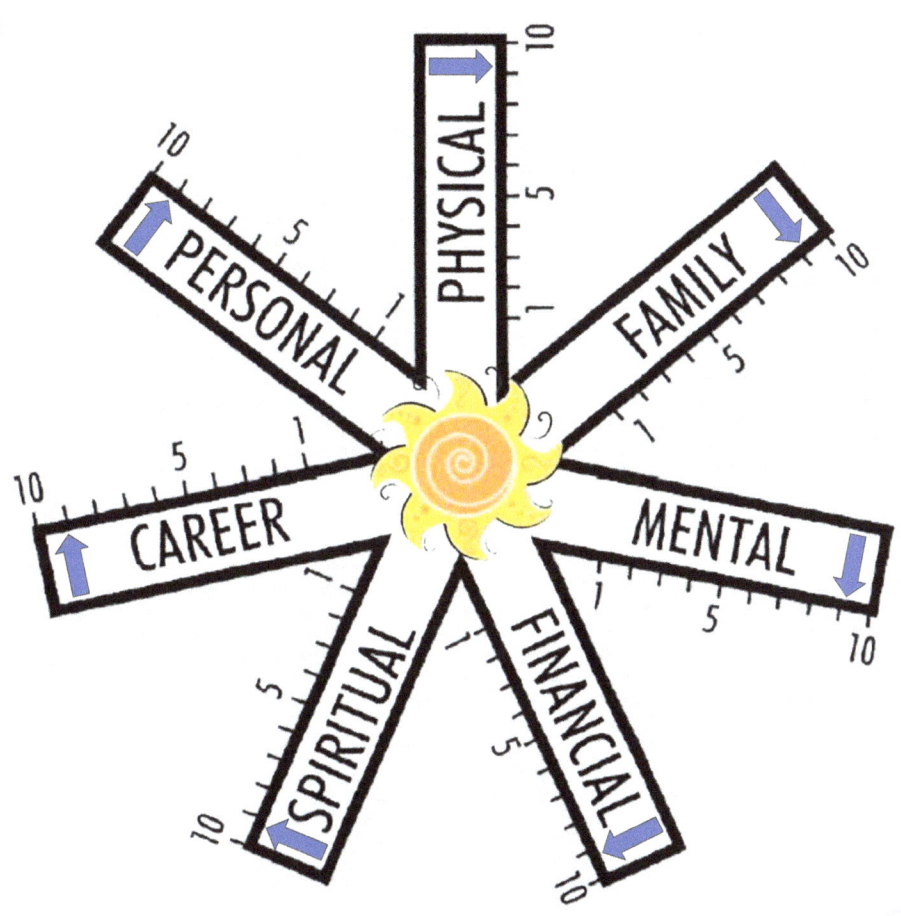

Take your scores from the previous page, plot your points, and color them in to see how your life is rolling!

Jot Down Your VISION For Each Spoke On Your Wheel of Life

Gratitude & Refelection
turn up the SUN LIGHT!

Be The Sunshine!

WHAT DO I SEE: MY VISION!

Our vision determines our direction as well as our OUTCOMES in life!
Spend some time writing in what you SEE for each area of your life

- PHYSICAL
- FAMILY
- MENTAL
- FINANCIAL
- SPIRITUAL
- CAREER
- PERSONAL

TODAY I WILL BE THE SUNSHINE!
DATE: January 1, 1999

RELATIONSHIPS I NEED TO CULTIVATE TODAY:

1- Dean
2- My Mother
3- Tyler Perry

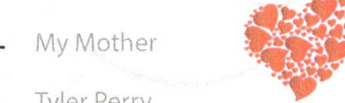

TODAY I AM GRATEFUL FOR:

Today I will call my brother Erik and FACETIME with Malena & Christopher. I also want to send a letter to my brothers Greg & Tony & my sister Sam.

MY INTENTION & COMMITMENT (ACTION STEPS) FOR THE DAY:

Today I am focused on healthy eating and feeling my best.

I have an exceptional relationship with husband.

I will write down my food intake and exercise at least 30 minutes.

Today I will cook a great dinner for my sweetheart.

Thoughts/Brilliant Ideas/Musings

I had a great start to my day- the afternoon was a bit blurry- perhaps I will try to adjust that tomorrow. I like the ideas I heard from the Leadership team today, perhaps I can create a Leadership WHY (White) Board for our next meeting?

REVISIT MY WINS TODAY (EVEN THE TINY ONES 😊)

I completed my workout, wrote down all of my food, made a great dinner, reached out to my Brother and got to see my niece and nephew on Facetime. I also had a great partnership call today with a potential referral partner.

WHAT DID I LEARN TODAY?

Today was a good day- if I had it to do over again, I would definitely schedule the time for the cards to my siblings so I was able to fit it in. I would also spend a bit more time planning the day ahead of time.

GOOD NIGHT THOUGHTS/PRAYERS:

Lord thank you for this AMAZING DAY!! I am excited for tomorrow and feel so very blessed for the many gifts in my life.

QUICK DAILY RATING:

 EXCEPTIONAL    PRETTY GOOD    AVERAGE    BACK TO THE DRAWING BOARD

Choose to shine.

TODAY I WILL BE THE SUNSHINE!
DATE:

RELATIONSHIPS I NEED TO CULTIVATE TODAY:

1-

2-

3-

TODAY I AM GRATEFUL FOR:

_____

_____

_____

MY INTENTION & COMMITMENT (ACTION STEPS) FOR THE DAY:

_____
_____
_____
_____

Thoughts/Brilliant Ideas/Musings

REVISIT MY WINS TODAY (EVEN THE TINY ONES 😊)

_____
_____

WHAT DID I LEARN TODAY?

_____
_____

GOOD NIGHT THOUGHTS/PRAYERS:

_____
_____
_____

QUICK DAILY RATING:

😍 EXCEPTIONAL   😀 PRETTY GOOD   😐 AVERAGE   😖 BACK TO THE DRAWING BOARD

A little Sun goes a long way.

TODAY I WILL BE THE SUNSHINE!
DATE:

**RELATIONSHIPS I
NEED TO CULTIVATE TODAY:**

TODAY I AM GRATEFUL FOR:

1-

2-

3-

MY INTENTION & COMMITMENT (ACTION STEPS) FOR THE DAY:

___

Thoughts/Brilliant Ideas/Musings

REVISIT MY WINS TODAY (EVEN THE TINY ONES 😊)

WHAT DID I LEARN TODAY?

GOOD NIGHT THOUGHTS/PRAYERS:

QUICK DAILY RATING:

😍 EXCEPTIONAL   😀 PRETTY GOOD   😐 AVERAGE   😖 BACK TO THE DRAWING BOARD

Be the change you wish to see. -Ghandi

TODAY I WILL BE THE SUNSHINE!
DATE:

RELATIONSHIPS I NEED TO CULTIVATE TODAY:

1-

2-

3-

TODAY I AM GRATEFUL FOR:

_____

_____

_____

MY INTENTION & COMMITMENT (ACTION STEPS) FOR THE DAY:

_____

_____

_____

Thoughts/Brilliant Ideas/Musings

REVISIT MY WINS TODAY (EVEN THE TINY ONES 😊)

_____

_____

WHAT DID I LEARN TODAY?

_____

_____

GOOD NIGHT THOUGHTS/PRAYERS:

_____

_____

_____

QUICK DAILY RATING:

😍 EXCEPTIONAL   😃 PRETTY GOOD   😐 AVERAGE   😣 BACK TO THE DRAWING BOARD

Light the way!

TODAY I WILL BE THE SUNSHINE!
DATE:

**RELATIONSHIPS I
NEED TO CULTIVATE TODAY:**

1-

2-

3-

TODAY I AM GRATEFUL FOR:

_____

_____

_____

MY INTENTION & COMMITMENT (ACTION STEPS) FOR THE DAY:

_____
_____
_____

Thoughts/Brilliant Ideas/Musings

REVISIT MY WINS TODAY (EVEN THE TINY ONES 😊)

_____
_____

WHAT DID I LEARN TODAY?

_____
_____

GOOD NIGHT THOUGHTS/PRAYERS:

_____
_____
_____

QUICK DAILY RATING:

🤩 EXCEPTIONAL   😄 PRETTY GOOD   😌 AVERAGE   😖 BACK TO THE DRAWING BOARD

Grateful, Thankful, Blessed!

TODAY I WILL BE THE SUNSHINE!
DATE:

**RELATIONSHIPS I
NEED TO CULTIVATE TODAY:**

TODAY I AM GRATEFUL FOR:

1-

2-

3-

_____

_____

_____

MY INTENTION & COMMITMENT (ACTION STEPS) FOR THE DAY:

_____
_____
_____

Thoughts/Brilliant Ideas/Musings

REVISIT MY WINS TODAY (EVEN THE TINY ONES 😊)
_____
_____

WHAT DID I LEARN TODAY?
_____
_____

GOOD NIGHT THOUGHTS/PRAYERS:
_____
_____
_____

QUICK DAILY RATING:

😍 EXCEPTIONAL   😃 PRETTY GOOD   🙂 AVERAGE   😖 BACK TO THE DRAWING BOARD

Sunshiny days are my favorite.

TODAY I WILL BE THE SUNSHINE!
DATE:

RELATIONSHIPS I NEED TO CULTIVATE TODAY:

1-

2-

3-

TODAY I AM GRATEFUL FOR:

_____

_____

_____

MY INTENTION & COMMITMENT (ACTION STEPS) FOR THE DAY:
_____
_____
_____

Thoughts/Brilliant Ideas/Musings

REVISIT MY WINS TODAY (EVEN THE TINY ONES 😊)
_____
_____

WHAT DID I LEARN TODAY?
_____
_____

GOOD NIGHT THOUGHTS/PRAYERS:
_____
_____
_____

QUICK DAILY RATING:

😍 EXCEPTIONAL 😄 PRETTY GOOD 😐 AVERAGE 😖 BACK TO THE DRAWING BOARD

Sunshine on my shoulders makes me happy.

TODAY I WILL BE THE SUNSHINE!
DATE:

**RELATIONSHIPS I
NEED TO CULTIVATE TODAY:**

TODAY I AM GRATEFUL FOR:

1-

2-

3-

_____

_____

_____

MY INTENTION & COMMITMENT (ACTION STEPS) FOR THE DAY:

_____

_____

_____

Thoughts/Brilliant Ideas/Musings

REVISIT MY WINS TODAY (EVEN THE TINY ONES 😊)

_____

_____

WHAT DID I LEARN TODAY?

_____

_____

GOOD NIGHT THOUGHTS/PRAYERS:

_____

_____

_____

QUICK DAILY RATING:

😍 EXCEPTIONAL   😃 PRETTY GOOD   😐 AVERAGE   😖 BACK TO THE DRAWING BOARD

Spread a little sunshine!

TODAY I WILL BE THE SUNSHINE!
DATE:

**RELATIONSHIPS I
NEED TO CULTIVATE TODAY:**

TODAY I AM GRATEFUL FOR:

1-

2-

3-

_____

_____

_____

MY INTENTION & COMMITMENT (ACTION STEPS) FOR THE DAY:
_____
_____
_____

Thoughts/Brilliant Ideas/Musings

REVISIT MY WINS TODAY (EVEN THE TINY ONES 😊)
_____
_____

WHAT DID I LEARN TODAY?
_____
_____

GOOD NIGHT THOUGHTS/PRAYERS:
_____
_____
_____

QUICK DAILY RATING:

😍 EXCEPTIONAL   😃 PRETTY GOOD   😐 AVERAGE   😖 BACK TO THE DRAWING BOARD

Rain makes the flowers grow.

TODAY I WILL BE THE SUNSHINE!
DATE:

**RELATIONSHIPS I
NEED TO CULTIVATE TODAY:**

TODAY I AM GRATEFUL FOR:

1-

2-

3-

MY INTENTION & COMMITMENT (ACTION STEPS) FOR THE DAY:
_____
_____
_____

Thoughts/Brilliant Ideas/Musings

REVISIT MY WINS TODAY (EVEN THE TINY ONES 😊)
_____
_____

WHAT DID I LEARN TODAY?
_____
_____

GOOD NIGHT THOUGHTS/PRAYERS:
_____
_____
_____

QUICK DAILY RATING:
😍 EXCEPTIONAL   😃 PRETTY GOOD   😐 AVERAGE   😖 BACK TO THE DRAWING BOARD

Sprinkle sunshine wherever you go.

TODAY I WILL BE THE SUNSHINE!
DATE:

**RELATIONSHIPS I
NEED TO CULTIVATE TODAY:**

TODAY I AM GRATEFUL FOR:

1-

2-

3-

_____

_____

_____

MY INTENTION & COMMITMENT (ACTION STEPS) FOR THE DAY:

_____
_____
_____

Thoughts/Brilliant Ideas/Musings

REVISIT MY WINS TODAY (EVEN THE TINY ONES 😊)

_____
_____

WHAT DID I LEARN TODAY?

_____
_____

GOOD NIGHT THOUGHTS/PRAYERS:

_____
_____
_____

QUICK DAILY RATING:

😍 EXCEPTIONAL   😁 PRETTY GOOD   😐 AVERAGE   😖 BACK TO THE DRAWING BOARD

Love is like sunshine.

TODAY I WILL BE THE SUNSHINE!
DATE:

RELATIONSHIPS I NEED TO CULTIVATE TODAY:

TODAY I AM GRATEFUL FOR:

1-

2-

3-

_____

_____

_____

MY INTENTION & COMMITMENT (ACTION STEPS) FOR THE DAY:

_____
_____
_____

Thoughts/Brilliant Ideas/Musings

REVISIT MY WINS TODAY (EVEN THE TINY ONES 😊)

_____
_____

WHAT DID I LEARN TODAY?

_____
_____

GOOD NIGHT THOUGHTS/PRAYERS:

_____
_____
_____

QUICK DAILY RATING:

😍 EXCEPTIONAL   😃 PRETTY GOOD   😐 AVERAGE   😖 BACK TO THE DRAWING BOARD

Wrap yourself in sunshine!

TODAY I WILL BE THE SUNSHINE!
DATE:

RELATIONSHIPS I NEED TO CULTIVATE TODAY:

1-

2-

3-

TODAY I AM GRATEFUL FOR:

_____

_____

_____

MY INTENTION & COMMITMENT (ACTION STEPS) FOR THE DAY:

_____
_____
_____

Thoughts/Brilliant Ideas/Musings

REVISIT MY WINS TODAY (EVEN THE TINY ONES 😊)
_____
_____

WHAT DID I LEARN TODAY?
_____
_____

GOOD NIGHT THOUGHTS/PRAYERS:
_____
_____
_____

QUICK DAILY RATING:

😍 EXCEPTIONAL   😀 PRETTY GOOD   😐 AVERAGE   😖 BACK TO THE DRAWING BOARD

BE the smile!

TODAY I WILL BE THE SUNSHINE!
DATE:

**RELATIONSHIPS I
NEED TO CULTIVATE TODAY:**

TODAY I AM GRATEFUL FOR:

1-

2-

3-

_____

_____

_____

MY INTENTION & COMMITMENT (ACTION STEPS) FOR THE DAY:

_____

_____

_____

Thoughts/Brilliant Ideas/Musings

REVISIT MY WINS TODAY (EVEN THE TINY ONES 😊)

_____

_____

WHAT DID I LEARN TODAY?

_____

_____

GOOD NIGHT THOUGHTS/PRAYERS:

_____

_____

_____

QUICK DAILY RATING:

😍 EXCEPTIONAL   😄 PRETTY GOOD   😐 AVERAGE   😖 BACK TO THE DRAWING BOARD

My future's so bright I gotta wear shades!

TODAY I WILL BE THE SUNSHINE!
DATE:

RELATIONSHIPS I NEED TO CULTIVATE TODAY:

TODAY I AM GRATEFUL FOR:

1-

2-

3-

_____

_____

_____

MY INTENTION & COMMITMENT (ACTION STEPS) FOR THE DAY:
_____
_____
_____

Thoughts/Brilliant Ideas/Musings

REVISIT MY WINS TODAY (EVEN THE TINY ONES 😊)
_____
_____

WHAT DID I LEARN TODAY?
_____
_____

GOOD NIGHT THOUGHTS/PRAYERS:
_____
_____
_____

QUICK DAILY RATING:

 EXCEPTIONAL  PRETTY GOOD  AVERAGE  BACK TO THE DRAWING BOARD

Live, Laugh, Love.

TODAY I WILL BE THE SUNSHINE!
DATE:

RELATIONSHIPS I NEED TO CULTIVATE TODAY:

TODAY I AM GRATEFUL FOR:

1-

2-

3-

MY INTENTION & COMMITMENT (ACTION STEPS) FOR THE DAY:

Thoughts/Brilliant Ideas/Musings

REVISIT MY WINS TODAY (EVEN THE TINY ONES 😊)

WHAT DID I LEARN TODAY?

GOOD NIGHT THOUGHTS/PRAYERS:

QUICK DAILY RATING:

😍 EXCEPTIONAL 😀 PRETTY GOOD 😐 AVERAGE 😖 BACK TO THE DRAWING BOARD

Plant today, grow tomorrow.

TODAY I WILL BE THE SUNSHINE!
DATE:

**RELATIONSHIPS I
NEED TO CULTIVATE TODAY:**

TODAY I AM GRATEFUL FOR:

1-

2-

3-

_____

_____

_____

MY INTENTION & COMMITMENT (ACTION STEPS) FOR THE DAY:
_____
_____
_____

Thoughts/Brilliant Ideas/Musings

REVISIT MY WINS TODAY (EVEN THE TINY ONES 😊)
_____
_____

WHAT DID I LEARN TODAY?
_____
_____

GOOD NIGHT THOUGHTS/PRAYERS:
_____
_____
_____

QUICK DAILY RATING:
😍 EXCEPTIONAL   😄 PRETTY GOOD   😐 AVERAGE   😖 BACK TO THE DRAWING BOARD

Take care of your people.

TODAY I WILL BE THE SUNSHINE!
DATE:

**RELATIONSHIPS I
NEED TO CULTIVATE TODAY:**

TODAY I AM GRATEFUL FOR:

1-

2-

3-

_____

_____

_____

MY INTENTION & COMMITMENT (ACTION STEPS) FOR THE DAY:

_____
_____
_____

Thoughts/Brilliant Ideas/Musings

REVISIT MY WINS TODAY (EVEN THE TINY ONES 😊)

_____
_____

WHAT DID I LEARN TODAY?

_____
_____

GOOD NIGHT THOUGHTS/PRAYERS:

_____
_____
_____

QUICK DAILY RATING:

😍 EXCEPTIONAL   😃 PRETTY GOOD   😐 AVERAGE   😖 BACK TO THE DRAWING BOARD

Tomorrow is not promised.

TODAY I WILL BE THE SUNSHINE!
DATE:

RELATIONSHIPS I NEED TO CULTIVATE TODAY:

1-

2-

3-

TODAY I AM GRATEFUL FOR:

_____

_____

_____

MY INTENTION & COMMITMENT (ACTION STEPS) FOR THE DAY:

_____
_____
_____

Thoughts/Brilliant Ideas/Musings

REVISIT MY WINS TODAY (EVEN THE TINY ONES 😊)

_____
_____

WHAT DID I LEARN TODAY?

_____
_____

GOOD NIGHT THOUGHTS/PRAYERS:

_____
_____
_____

QUICK DAILY RATING:

😍 EXCEPTIONAL　　😃 PRETTY GOOD　　😐 AVERAGE　　😖 BACK TO THE DRAWING BOARD

Make the most of today.

TODAY I WILL BE THE SUNSHINE!
DATE:

RELATIONSHIPS I NEED TO CULTIVATE TODAY:

TODAY I AM GRATEFUL FOR:

1-

2-

3-

MY INTENTION & COMMITMENT (ACTION STEPS) FOR THE DAY:

Thoughts/Brilliant Ideas/Musings

REVISIT MY WINS TODAY (EVEN THE TINY ONES 😊)

WHAT DID I LEARN TODAY?

GOOD NIGHT THOUGHTS/PRAYERS:

QUICK DAILY RATING:

🤩 EXCEPTIONAL   😀 PRETTY GOOD   😔 AVERAGE   😖 BACK TO THE DRAWING BOARD

Watch a sunset.

TODAY I WILL BE THE SUNSHINE!
DATE:

**RELATIONSHIPS I
NEED TO CULTIVATE TODAY:**

1-

2-

3-

TODAY I AM GRATEFUL FOR:

_____

_____

_____

MY INTENTION & COMMITMENT (ACTION STEPS) FOR THE DAY:

_____
_____
_____
_____

Thoughts/Brilliant Ideas/Musings

REVISIT MY WINS TODAY (EVEN THE TINY ONES 😊)

_____
_____

WHAT DID I LEARN TODAY?

_____
_____

GOOD NIGHT THOUGHTS/PRAYERS:

_____
_____
_____

QUICK DAILY RATING:

😍 EXCEPTIONAL   😄 PRETTY GOOD   😌 AVERAGE   😖 BACK TO THE DRAWING BOARD

Get up for the sunrise.

TODAY I WILL BE THE SUNSHINE!
DATE:

RELATIONSHIPS I NEED TO CULTIVATE TODAY:

1-

2-

3-

TODAY I AM GRATEFUL FOR:

_____

_____

_____

MY INTENTION & COMMITMENT (ACTION STEPS) FOR THE DAY:

_____
_____
_____

Thoughts/Brilliant Ideas/Musings

REVISIT MY WINS TODAY (EVEN THE TINY ONES 😊)
_____
_____

WHAT DID I LEARN TODAY?
_____
_____

GOOD NIGHT THOUGHTS/PRAYERS:
_____
_____
_____

QUICK DAILY RATING:

😍 EXCEPTIONAL   😃 PRETTY GOOD   😐 AVERAGE   😖 BACK TO THE DRAWING BOARD

Yes- YOU CAN!

TODAY I WILL BE THE SUNSHINE!
DATE:

**RELATIONSHIPS I
NEED TO CULTIVATE TODAY:**

TODAY I AM GRATEFUL FOR:

1-

2-

3-

MY INTENTION & COMMITMENT (ACTION STEPS) FOR THE DAY:

_____
_____
_____

Thoughts/Brilliant Ideas/Musings

REVISIT MY WINS TODAY (EVEN THE TINY ONES 😊)
_____
_____

WHAT DID I LEARN TODAY?
_____
_____

GOOD NIGHT THOUGHTS/PRAYERS:
_____
_____
_____

QUICK DAILY RATING:

😍 EXCEPTIONAL   😀 PRETTY GOOD   😐 AVERAGE   😖 BACK TO THE DRAWING BOARD

Love with all your heart.

TODAY I WILL BE THE SUNSHINE!
DATE:

RELATIONSHIPS I NEED TO CULTIVATE TODAY:

TODAY I AM GRATEFUL FOR:

1-

2-

3-

MY INTENTION & COMMITMENT (ACTION STEPS) FOR THE DAY:

Thoughts/Brilliant Ideas/Musings

REVISIT MY WINS TODAY (EVEN THE TINY ONES 😊)

WHAT DID I LEARN TODAY?

GOOD NIGHT THOUGHTS/PRAYERS:

QUICK DAILY RATING:

 EXCEPTIONAL    PRETTY GOOD   😔 AVERAGE   BACK TO THE DRAWING BOARD

Cherish your wins.

TODAY I WILL BE THE SUNSHINE!
DATE:

**RELATIONSHIPS I
NEED TO CULTIVATE TODAY:**

TODAY I AM GRATEFUL FOR:

1-

2-

3-

_____

_____

_____

MY INTENTION & COMMITMENT (ACTION STEPS) FOR THE DAY:
_____
_____
_____

Thoughts/Brilliant Ideas/Musings

REVISIT MY WINS TODAY (EVEN THE TINY ONES 😊)
_____
_____

WHAT DID I LEARN TODAY?
_____
_____

GOOD NIGHT THOUGHTS/PRAYERS:
_____
_____
_____

QUICK DAILY RATING:

😍 EXCEPTIONAL 😃 PRETTY GOOD 😐 AVERAGE 😖 BACK TO THE DRAWING BOARD

Spend every minute wisely.

TODAY I WILL BE THE SUNSHINE!
DATE:

**RELATIONSHIPS I
NEED TO CULTIVATE TODAY:**

TODAY I AM GRATEFUL FOR:

1-

2-

3-

_____

_____

_____

MY INTENTION & COMMITMENT (ACTION STEPS) FOR THE DAY:

_____

_____

_____

Thoughts/Brilliant Ideas/Musings

REVISIT MY WINS TODAY (EVEN THE TINY ONES 😊)

_____

_____

WHAT DID I LEARN TODAY?

_____

_____

GOOD NIGHT THOUGHTS/PRAYERS:

_____

_____

_____

QUICK DAILY RATING:

😍 EXCEPTIONAL   😀 PRETTY GOOD   🙂 AVERAGE   😣 BACK TO THE DRAWING BOARD

A penny for your thoughts.

TODAY I WILL BE THE SUNSHINE!
DATE:

RELATIONSHIPS I NEED TO CULTIVATE TODAY:

TODAY I AM GRATEFUL FOR:

1-

2-

3-

MY INTENTION & COMMITMENT (ACTION STEPS) FOR THE DAY:

_____
_____
_____

Thoughts/Brilliant Ideas/Musings

REVISIT MY WINS TODAY (EVEN THE TINY ONES 😊)
_____
_____

WHAT DID I LEARN TODAY?
_____
_____

GOOD NIGHT THOUGHTS/PRAYERS:
_____
_____

QUICK DAILY RATING:

😍 EXCEPTIONAL   😃 PRETTY GOOD   😐 AVERAGE   😖 BACK TO THE DRAWING BOARD

YOU got this!

TODAY I WILL BE THE SUNSHINE!

DATE:

RELATIONSHIPS I NEED TO CULTIVATE TODAY:

TODAY I AM GRATEFUL FOR:

1-

2-

3-

MY INTENTION & COMMITMENT (ACTION STEPS) FOR THE DAY:

Thoughts/Brilliant Ideas/Musings

REVISIT MY WINS TODAY (EVEN THE TINY ONES 😊)

WHAT DID I LEARN TODAY?

GOOD NIGHT THOUGHTS/PRAYERS:

QUICK DAILY RATING:

😍 EXCEPTIONAL   😃 PRETTY GOOD   😐 AVERAGE   😣 BACK TO THE DRAWING BOARD

Plan for success.

TODAY I WILL BE THE SUNSHINE!
DATE:

RELATIONSHIPS I NEED TO CULTIVATE TODAY:

1-

2-

3-

TODAY I AM GRATEFUL FOR:

_____

_____

_____

MY INTENTION & COMMITMENT (ACTION STEPS) FOR THE DAY:
_____
_____
_____

Thoughts/Brilliant Ideas/Musings

REVISIT MY WINS TODAY (EVEN THE TINY ONES 😊)
_____
_____

WHAT DID I LEARN TODAY?
_____
_____

GOOD NIGHT THOUGHTS/PRAYERS:
_____
_____
_____

QUICK DAILY RATING:

😍 EXCEPTIONAL   😃 PRETTY GOOD   😐 AVERAGE   😖 BACK TO THE DRAWING BOARD

Water your soul.

TODAY I WILL BE THE SUNSHINE!
DATE:

RELATIONSHIPS I NEED TO CULTIVATE TODAY:

1-

2-

3-

TODAY I AM GRATEFUL FOR:

_____

_____

_____

MY INTENTION & COMMITMENT (ACTION STEPS) FOR THE DAY:

_____

_____

_____

Thoughts/Brilliant Ideas/Musings

REVISIT MY WINS TODAY (EVEN THE TINY ONES 😊)

_____

_____

WHAT DID I LEARN TODAY?

_____

_____

GOOD NIGHT THOUGHTS/PRAYERS:

_____

_____

_____

QUICK DAILY RATING:

😍 EXCEPTIONAL   😃 PRETTY GOOD   😐 AVERAGE   😖 BACK TO THE DRAWING BOARD

Stop to smell the flowers.

TODAY I WILL BE THE SUNSHINE!
DATE:

RELATIONSHIPS I NEED TO CULTIVATE TODAY:

1-

2-

3-

TODAY I AM GRATEFUL FOR:

_____

_____

_____

MY INTENTION & COMMITMENT (ACTION STEPS) FOR THE DAY:

_____
_____
_____

Thoughts/Brilliant Ideas/Musings

REVISIT MY WINS TODAY (EVEN THE TINY ONES 😊)

_____
_____

WHAT DID I LEARN TODAY?

_____
_____

GOOD NIGHT THOUGHTS/PRAYERS:

_____
_____
_____

QUICK DAILY RATING:

😍 EXCEPTIONAL   😃 PRETTY GOOD   😐 AVERAGE   😖 BACK TO THE DRAWING BOARD

You get what you tolerate.

TODAY I WILL BE THE SUNSHINE!

DATE:

RELATIONSHIPS I NEED TO CULTIVATE TODAY:

1-

2-

3-

TODAY I AM GRATEFUL FOR:

_____

_____

_____

MY INTENTION & COMMITMENT (ACTION STEPS) FOR THE DAY:

_____

_____

_____

Thoughts/Brilliant Ideas/Musings

REVISIT MY WINS TODAY (EVEN THE TINY ONES 😊)

_____

_____

WHAT DID I LEARN TODAY?

_____

_____

GOOD NIGHT THOUGHTS/PRAYERS:

_____

_____

_____

QUICK DAILY RATING:

😍 EXCEPTIONAL   😁 PRETTY GOOD   😌 AVERAGE   😖 BACK TO THE DRAWING BOARD

Love always wins!

Be The Sunshine!

30-DAY REFLECTION

TODAY I AM GRATEFUL FOR: Over the past 30 days—did I see any patterns?

RELATIONSHIPS I NEED TO CULTIVATE: Did I see an improvement in my relationships, and are there relationships I want to cultivate in the next 30 days?

MY INTENTIONS: What did I accomplish in the past 30 days related to my intentions, and are there other areas where I need to focus?

REVISIT MY WINS: Review your wins for the past 30 days! CONGRATS!

DO OVER: What will I do differently in my next 30 days?

QUICK DAILY RATING: What was your AVERAGE score over the past 30 days—reflect on that rating!

Am I <u>moving closer to</u> or <u>further away from</u> my vision? Check the vision page (page 10).

Gratitude & Reflection turn up the SUN LIGHT!

Be The Sunshine!

DO YOU KNOW SOMEONE WHO WOULD ENJOY HAVING A GRATITUDE JOURNAL?

 Order your journals here and share your experience!

Gratitude & Refelection turn up the SUN LIGHT!

TODAY I WILL BE THE SUNSHINE!

DATE:

RELATIONSHIPS I NEED TO CULTIVATE TODAY:

1-

2-

3-

TODAY I AM GRATEFUL FOR:

_____

_____

_____

MY INTENTION & COMMITMENT (ACTION STEPS) FOR THE DAY:

_____
_____
_____

Thoughts/Brilliant Ideas/Musings

REVISIT MY WINS TODAY (EVEN THE TINY ONES 😊)

_____
_____

WHAT DID I LEARN TODAY?

_____
_____

GOOD NIGHT THOUGHTS/PRAYERS:

_____
_____
_____

QUICK DAILY RATING:

😍 EXCEPTIONAL   😁 PRETTY GOOD   😐 AVERAGE   😖 BACK TO THE DRAWING BOARD

Happiness is not a destination; it's a way of life.

TODAY I WILL BE THE SUNSHINE!

DATE:

RELATIONSHIPS I NEED TO CULTIVATE TODAY:

1-

2-

3-

TODAY I AM GRATEFUL FOR:

_____

_____

_____

MY INTENTION & COMMITMENT (ACTION STEPS) FOR THE DAY:

_____
_____
_____

Thoughts/Brilliant Ideas/Musings

REVISIT MY WINS TODAY (EVEN THE TINY ONES 😊)
_____
_____

WHAT DID I LEARN TODAY?
_____
_____

GOOD NIGHT THOUGHTS/PRAYERS:
_____
_____
_____

QUICK DAILY RATING:

😍 EXCEPTIONAL   😃 PRETTY GOOD   🙂 AVERAGE   😖 BACK TO THE DRAWING BOARD

Sunshine is the best medicine.

TODAY I WILL BE THE SUNSHINE!
DATE:

RELATIONSHIPS I NEED TO CULTIVATE TODAY:

1-

2-

3-

TODAY I AM GRATEFUL FOR:

_____
_____
_____

MY INTENTION & COMMITMENT (ACTION STEPS) FOR THE DAY:

_____
_____
_____
_____

Thoughts/Brilliant Ideas/Musings

REVISIT MY WINS TODAY (EVEN THE TINY ONES 😊)

_____
_____

WHAT DID I LEARN TODAY?

_____
_____

GOOD NIGHT THOUGHTS/PRAYERS:

_____
_____
_____

QUICK DAILY RATING:

😎 EXCEPTIONAL   😃 PRETTY GOOD   😐 AVERAGE   😖 BACK TO THE DRAWING BOARD

Choose happiness every day.

TODAY I WILL BE THE SUNSHINE!
DATE:

**RELATIONSHIPS I
NEED TO CULTIVATE TODAY:**

1-

2-

3-

TODAY I AM GRATEFUL FOR:

_____

_____

_____

MY INTENTION & COMMITMENT (ACTION STEPS) FOR THE DAY:

_____

_____

_____

Thoughts/Brilliant Ideas/Musings

REVISIT MY WINS TODAY (EVEN THE TINY ONES 😊)

_____

_____

WHAT DID I LEARN TODAY?

_____

_____

GOOD NIGHT THOUGHTS/PRAYERS:

_____

_____

_____

QUICK DAILY RATING:

😍 EXCEPTIONAL   😀 PRETTY GOOD   🙂 AVERAGE   😖 BACK TO THE DRAWING BOARD

A happy heart makes the face cheerful.

TODAY I WILL BE THE SUNSHINE!
DATE:

RELATIONSHIPS I NEED TO CULTIVATE TODAY:

1-

2-

3-

TODAY I AM GRATEFUL FOR:

_____

_____

_____

MY INTENTION & COMMITMENT (ACTION STEPS) FOR THE DAY:

_____

_____

_____

Thoughts/Brilliant Ideas/Musings

REVISIT MY WINS TODAY (EVEN THE TINY ONES 😊)

_____

_____

WHAT DID I LEARN TODAY?

_____

_____

GOOD NIGHT THOUGHTS/PRAYERS:

_____

_____

_____

QUICK DAILY RATING:

😍 EXCEPTIONAL   😄 PRETTY GOOD   😐 AVERAGE   😖 BACK TO THE DRAWING BOARD

Find joy in the ordinary.

TODAY I WILL BE THE SUNSHINE!
DATE:

RELATIONSHIPS I NEED TO CULTIVATE TODAY:

1-

2-

3-

TODAY I AM GRATEFUL FOR:

_____

_____

_____

MY INTENTION & COMMITMENT (ACTION STEPS) FOR THE DAY:

_____
_____
_____

Thoughts/Brilliant Ideas/Musings

REVISIT MY WINS TODAY (EVEN THE TINY ONES 😊)

_____
_____

WHAT DID I LEARN TODAY?

_____
_____

GOOD NIGHT THOUGHTS/PRAYERS:

_____
_____
_____

QUICK DAILY RATING:

 EXCEPTIONAL    PRETTY GOOD    AVERAGE    BACK TO THE DRAWING BOARD

Sunshine mixed with a little hurricane.

TODAY I WILL BE THE SUNSHINE!
DATE:

RELATIONSHIPS I NEED TO CULTIVATE TODAY:

1-

2-

3-

TODAY I AM GRATEFUL FOR:

_____

_____

_____

MY INTENTION & COMMITMENT (ACTION STEPS) FOR THE DAY:

_____

_____

_____

Thoughts/Brilliant Ideas/Musings

REVISIT MY WINS TODAY (EVEN THE TINY ONES 😊)

_____

_____

WHAT DID I LEARN TODAY?

_____

_____

GOOD NIGHT THOUGHTS/PRAYERS:

_____

_____

_____

QUICK DAILY RATING:

😍 EXCEPTIONAL 😄 PRETTY GOOD 😐 AVERAGE 😖 BACK TO THE DRAWING BOARD

The sun always shines above the clouds.

TODAY I WILL BE THE SUNSHINE!
DATE:

**RELATIONSHIPS I
NEED TO CULTIVATE TODAY:**

TODAY I AM GRATEFUL FOR:

1-

2-

3-

___

MY INTENTION & COMMITMENT (ACTION STEPS) FOR THE DAY:

___

Thoughts/Brilliant Ideas/Musings

REVISIT MY WINS TODAY (EVEN THE TINY ONES 😊)

___

WHAT DID I LEARN TODAY?

___

GOOD NIGHT THOUGHTS/PRAYERS:

___

QUICK DAILY RATING:

😍 EXCEPTIONAL   😃 PRETTY GOOD   😐 AVERAGE   😖 BACK TO THE DRAWING BOARD

Happiness is a warm cup of coffee and a good book.

TODAY I WILL BE THE SUNSHINE!
DATE:

RELATIONSHIPS I NEED TO CULTIVATE TODAY:

1-

2-

3-

TODAY I AM GRATEFUL FOR:

_____

_____

_____

MY INTENTION & COMMITMENT (ACTION STEPS) FOR THE DAY:

_____

_____

_____

Thoughts/Brilliant Ideas/Musings

REVISIT MY WINS TODAY (EVEN THE TINY ONES 😊)

_____

_____

WHAT DID I LEARN TODAY?

_____

_____

GOOD NIGHT THOUGHTS/PRAYERS:

_____

_____

_____

QUICK DAILY RATING:

😍 EXCEPTIONAL   😄 PRETTY GOOD   😐 AVERAGE   😖 BACK TO THE DRAWING BOARD

Smile, it's free therapy.

TODAY I WILL BE THE SUNSHINE!
DATE:

RELATIONSHIPS I NEED TO CULTIVATE TODAY:

1-

2-

3-

TODAY I AM GRATEFUL FOR:

_____

_____

_____

MY INTENTION & COMMITMENT (ACTION STEPS) FOR THE DAY:

_____
_____
_____

Thoughts/Brilliant Ideas/Musings

REVISIT MY WINS TODAY (EVEN THE TINY ONES 😊)
_____
_____

WHAT DID I LEARN TODAY?
_____
_____

GOOD NIGHT THOUGHTS/PRAYERS:
_____
_____
_____

QUICK DAILY RATING:

😍 EXCEPTIONAL   😀 PRETTY GOOD   😐 AVERAGE   😖 BACK TO THE DRAWING BOARD

Sunshine is the key to my heart.

TODAY I WILL BE THE SUNSHINE!
DATE:

RELATIONSHIPS I NEED TO CULTIVATE TODAY:

1-

2-

3-

TODAY I AM GRATEFUL FOR:

_____

_____

_____

MY INTENTION & COMMITMENT (ACTION STEPS) FOR THE DAY:

_____
_____
_____

Thoughts/Brilliant Ideas/Musings

REVISIT MY WINS TODAY (EVEN THE TINY ONES 😊)

_____
_____

WHAT DID I LEARN TODAY?

_____
_____

GOOD NIGHT THOUGHTS/PRAYERS:

_____
_____
_____

QUICK DAILY RATING:

😍 EXCEPTIONAL   😃 PRETTY GOOD   🙂 AVERAGE   😖 BACK TO THE DRAWING BOARD

Happiness is homemade.

TODAY I WILL BE THE SUNSHINE!
DATE:

**RELATIONSHIPS I
NEED TO CULTIVATE TODAY:**

TODAY I AM GRATEFUL FOR:

1-

2-

3-

MY INTENTION & COMMITMENT (ACTION STEPS) FOR THE DAY:

___

Thoughts/Brilliant Ideas/Musings

REVISIT MY WINS TODAY (EVEN THE TINY ONES 😊)

WHAT DID I LEARN TODAY?

GOOD NIGHT THOUGHTS/PRAYERS:

QUICK DAILY RATING:

😍 EXCEPTIONAL　　😄 PRETTY GOOD　　🙂 AVERAGE　　😖 BACK TO THE DRAWING BOARD

The sun sees your body, but the sunshine sees your soul.

TODAY I WILL BE THE SUNSHINE!
DATE:

**RELATIONSHIPS I
NEED TO CULTIVATE TODAY:**

TODAY I AM GRATEFUL FOR:

1-

2-

3-

MY INTENTION & COMMITMENT (ACTION STEPS) FOR THE DAY:
___
___
___

Thoughts/Brilliant Ideas/Musings

REVISIT MY WINS TODAY (EVEN THE TINY ONES 😊)
___
___

WHAT DID I LEARN TODAY?
___
___

GOOD NIGHT THOUGHTS/PRAYERS:
___
___
___

QUICK DAILY RATING:
😍 EXCEPTIONAL   😄 PRETTY GOOD   😐 AVERAGE   😖 BACK TO THE DRAWING BOARD

Let your joy be in your journey,
not in some distant goal.

TODAY I WILL BE THE SUNSHINE!
DATE:

RELATIONSHIPS I NEED TO CULTIVATE TODAY:

1-

2-

3-

TODAY I AM GRATEFUL FOR:
_____
_____
_____

MY INTENTION & COMMITMENT (ACTION STEPS) FOR THE DAY:
_____
_____
_____

Thoughts/Brilliant Ideas/Musings

REVISIT MY WINS TODAY (EVEN THE TINY ONES 😊)
_____
_____

WHAT DID I LEARN TODAY?
_____
_____

GOOD NIGHT THOUGHTS/PRAYERS:
_____
_____
_____

QUICK DAILY RATING:

😍 EXCEPTIONAL   😃 PRETTY GOOD   😐 AVERAGE   😖 BACK TO THE DRAWING BOARD

Sunshine is a state of mind.

TODAY I WILL BE THE SUNSHINE!
DATE:

RELATIONSHIPS I NEED TO CULTIVATE TODAY:

1-

2-

3-

TODAY I AM GRATEFUL FOR:

_____

_____

_____

MY INTENTION & COMMITMENT (ACTION STEPS) FOR THE DAY:

_____
_____
_____

Thoughts/Brilliant Ideas/Musings

REVISIT MY WINS TODAY (EVEN THE TINY ONES 😊)
_____
_____

WHAT DID I LEARN TODAY?
_____
_____

GOOD NIGHT THOUGHTS/PRAYERS:
_____
_____
_____

QUICK DAILY RATING:

😍 EXCEPTIONAL   😃 PRETTY GOOD   😐 AVERAGE   😣 BACK TO THE DRAWING BOARD

Happiness is a choice, not a result.

TODAY I WILL BE THE SUNSHINE!
DATE:

**RELATIONSHIPS I
NEED TO CULTIVATE TODAY:**

TODAY I AM GRATEFUL FOR:

1-

2-

3-

_____
_____
_____

MY INTENTION & COMMITMENT (ACTION STEPS) FOR THE DAY:
_____
_____
_____

Thoughts/Brilliant Ideas/Musings

REVISIT MY WINS TODAY (EVEN THE TINY ONES 😊)
_____
_____

WHAT DID I LEARN TODAY?
_____
_____

GOOD NIGHT THOUGHTS/PRAYERS:
_____
_____
_____

QUICK DAILY RATING:
😍 EXCEPTIONAL   😃 PRETTY GOOD   😐 AVERAGE   😖 BACK TO THE DRAWING BOARD

Don't worry, be happy.

TODAY I WILL BE THE SUNSHINE!
DATE:

**RELATIONSHIPS I
NEED TO CULTIVATE TODAY:**

TODAY I AM GRATEFUL FOR:

1-

2-

3-

MY INTENTION & COMMITMENT (ACTION STEPS) FOR THE DAY:
___
___
___

Thoughts/Brilliant Ideas/Musings

REVISIT MY WINS TODAY (EVEN THE TINY ONES 😊)
___
___

WHAT DID I LEARN TODAY?
___
___

GOOD NIGHT THOUGHTS/PRAYERS:
___
___
___

QUICK DAILY RATING:
 EXCEPTIONAL    PRETTY GOOD    AVERAGE    BACK TO THE DRAWING BOARD

Sunshine is the best accessory.

TODAY I WILL BE THE SUNSHINE!
DATE:

**RELATIONSHIPS I
NEED TO CULTIVATE TODAY:**

TODAY I AM GRATEFUL FOR:

1-

2-

3-

MY INTENTION & COMMITMENT (ACTION STEPS) FOR THE DAY:

_____
_____
_____

Thoughts/Brilliant Ideas/Musings

REVISIT MY WINS TODAY (EVEN THE TINY ONES 😊)
_____
_____

WHAT DID I LEARN TODAY?
_____
_____

GOOD NIGHT THOUGHTS/PRAYERS:
_____
_____
_____

QUICK DAILY RATING:

😍 EXCEPTIONAL   😃 PRETTY GOOD   😐 AVERAGE   😖 BACK TO THE DRAWING BOARD

The sun is a daily reminder that we too can rise again from the darkness.

TODAY I WILL BE THE SUNSHINE!
DATE:

**RELATIONSHIPS I
NEED TO CULTIVATE TODAY:**   **TODAY I AM GRATEFUL FOR:**

1- _____

2- _____

3- _____

MY INTENTION & COMMITMENT (ACTION STEPS) FOR THE DAY:
_____
_____
_____

Thoughts/Brilliant Ideas/Musings

REVISIT MY WINS TODAY (EVEN THE TINY ONES 😊)
_____
_____

WHAT DID I LEARN TODAY?
_____
_____

GOOD NIGHT THOUGHTS/PRAYERS:
_____
_____
_____

QUICK DAILY RATING:
😍 EXCEPTIONAL   😀 PRETTY GOOD   😐 AVERAGE   😖 BACK TO THE DRAWING BOARD

Be the reason someone smiles today.

TODAY I WILL BE THE SUNSHINE!
DATE:

RELATIONSHIPS I NEED TO CULTIVATE TODAY:

1-

2-

3-

TODAY I AM GRATEFUL FOR:

_____

_____

_____

MY INTENTION & COMMITMENT (ACTION STEPS) FOR THE DAY:

_____
_____
_____

Thoughts/Brilliant Ideas/Musings

REVISIT MY WINS TODAY (EVEN THE TINY ONES 😊)

_____
_____

WHAT DID I LEARN TODAY?

_____
_____

GOOD NIGHT THOUGHTS/PRAYERS:

_____
_____
_____

QUICK DAILY RATING:

 EXCEPTIONAL    PRETTY GOOD   😐 AVERAGE    BACK TO THE DRAWING BOARD

A day without laughter is a day wasted.

TODAY I WILL BE THE SUNSHINE!
DATE:

RELATIONSHIPS I NEED TO CULTIVATE TODAY:

1-

2-

3-

TODAY I AM GRATEFUL FOR:

_____

_____

_____

MY INTENTION & COMMITMENT (ACTION STEPS) FOR THE DAY:

_____

_____

_____

Thoughts/Brilliant Ideas/Musings

REVISIT MY WINS TODAY (EVEN THE TINY ONES 😊)

_____

_____

WHAT DID I LEARN TODAY?

_____

_____

GOOD NIGHT THOUGHTS/PRAYERS:

_____

_____

_____

QUICK DAILY RATING:

😍 EXCEPTIONAL　　😄 PRETTY GOOD　　😊 AVERAGE　　😖 BACK TO THE DRAWING BOARD

Chase the sun, not the storm.

TODAY I WILL BE THE SUNSHINE!
DATE:

RELATIONSHIPS I NEED TO CULTIVATE TODAY:

1-

2-

3-

TODAY I AM GRATEFUL FOR:

_____

_____

_____

MY INTENTION & COMMITMENT (ACTION STEPS) FOR THE DAY:

_____
_____
_____

Thoughts/Brilliant Ideas/Musings

REVISIT MY WINS TODAY (EVEN THE TINY ONES 😊)

_____
_____

WHAT DID I LEARN TODAY?

_____
_____

GOOD NIGHT THOUGHTS/PRAYERS:

_____
_____
_____

QUICK DAILY RATING:

😍 EXCEPTIONAL   😃 PRETTY GOOD   😐 AVERAGE   😖 BACK TO THE DRAWING BOARD

Happiness blooms from within.

TODAY I WILL BE THE SUNSHINE!
DATE:

**RELATIONSHIPS I
NEED TO CULTIVATE TODAY:**

TODAY I AM GRATEFUL FOR:

1-

2-

3-

_____

_____

_____

MY INTENTION & COMMITMENT (ACTION STEPS) FOR THE DAY:

_____
_____
_____

Thoughts/Brilliant Ideas/Musings

REVISIT MY WINS TODAY (EVEN THE TINY ONES 😊)

_____
_____

WHAT DID I LEARN TODAY?

_____
_____

GOOD NIGHT THOUGHTS/PRAYERS:

_____
_____
_____

QUICK DAILY RATING:

😍 EXCEPTIONAL   😃 PRETTY GOOD   😐 AVERAGE   😖 BACK TO THE DRAWING BOARD

Keep your face always toward the sunshine—and shadows will fall behind you.

TODAY I WILL BE THE SUNSHINE!
DATE:

**RELATIONSHIPS I
NEED TO CULTIVATE TODAY:**

1-

2-

3-

TODAY I AM GRATEFUL FOR:

_____

_____

_____

MY INTENTION & COMMITMENT (ACTION STEPS) FOR THE DAY:

_____

_____

_____

Thoughts/Brilliant Ideas/Musings

REVISIT MY WINS TODAY (EVEN THE TINY ONES 😊)

_____

_____

WHAT DID I LEARN TODAY?

_____

_____

GOOD NIGHT THOUGHTS/PRAYERS:

_____

_____

_____

QUICK DAILY RATING:

😍 EXCEPTIONAL   😃 PRETTY GOOD   😌 AVERAGE   😖 BACK TO THE DRAWING BOARD

Happiness is the secret to all beauty;
there is no beauty without happiness.

TODAY I WILL BE THE SUNSHINE!
DATE:

**RELATIONSHIPS I
NEED TO CULTIVATE TODAY:**

TODAY I AM GRATEFUL FOR:

1-

2-

3-

MY INTENTION & COMMITMENT (ACTION STEPS) FOR THE DAY:
_____
_____
_____

Thoughts/Brilliant Ideas/Musings

REVISIT MY WINS TODAY (EVEN THE TINY ONES 😊)
_____
_____

WHAT DID I LEARN TODAY?
_____
_____

GOOD NIGHT THOUGHTS/PRAYERS:
_____
_____

QUICK DAILY RATING:
😍 EXCEPTIONAL   😁 PRETTY GOOD   😐 AVERAGE   😖 BACK TO THE DRAWING BOARD

Sunshine is the art of thinking positively.

TODAY I WILL BE THE SUNSHINE!
DATE:

RELATIONSHIPS I NEED TO CULTIVATE TODAY:

1-

2-

3-

TODAY I AM GRATEFUL FOR:

_____

_____

_____

MY INTENTION & COMMITMENT (ACTION STEPS) FOR THE DAY:

_____

_____

_____

Thoughts/Brilliant Ideas/Musings

REVISIT MY WINS TODAY (EVEN THE TINY ONES 😊)

_____

_____

WHAT DID I LEARN TODAY?

_____

_____

GOOD NIGHT THOUGHTS/PRAYERS:

_____

_____

_____

QUICK DAILY RATING:

 EXCEPTIONAL  PRETTY GOOD  AVERAGE  BACK TO THE DRAWING BOARD

Find joy in the journey, not the destination.

TODAY I WILL BE THE SUNSHINE!
DATE:

**RELATIONSHIPS I
NEED TO CULTIVATE TODAY:**

TODAY I AM GRATEFUL FOR:

1-

2-

3-

_____

_____

_____

MY INTENTION & COMMITMENT (ACTION STEPS) FOR THE DAY:

_____
_____
_____

Thoughts/Brilliant Ideas/Musings

REVISIT MY WINS TODAY (EVEN THE TINY ONES 😊)

_____
_____

WHAT DID I LEARN TODAY?

_____
_____

GOOD NIGHT THOUGHTS/PRAYERS:

_____
_____
_____

QUICK DAILY RATING:

 EXCEPTIONAL    PRETTY GOOD    AVERAGE    BACK TO THE DRAWING BOARD

*Happiness is contagious,
spread it like confetti.*

TODAY I WILL BE THE SUNSHINE!
DATE:

RELATIONSHIPS I NEED TO CULTIVATE TODAY:

1-

2-

3-

TODAY I AM GRATEFUL FOR:

_____

_____

_____

MY INTENTION & COMMITMENT (ACTION STEPS) FOR THE DAY:

_____

_____

_____

Thoughts/Brilliant Ideas/Musings

REVISIT MY WINS TODAY (EVEN THE TINY ONES 😊)

_____

_____

WHAT DID I LEARN TODAY?

_____

_____

GOOD NIGHT THOUGHTS/PRAYERS:

_____

_____

_____

QUICK DAILY RATING:

😍 EXCEPTIONAL   😃 PRETTY GOOD   🙂 AVERAGE   😖 BACK TO THE DRAWING BOARD

Life is better when you're laughing.

TODAY I WILL BE THE SUNSHINE!
DATE:

RELATIONSHIPS I NEED TO CULTIVATE TODAY:

TODAY I AM GRATEFUL FOR:

1-

2-

3-

MY INTENTION & COMMITMENT (ACTION STEPS) FOR THE DAY:
___
___
___

Thoughts/Brilliant Ideas/Musings

REVISIT MY WINS TODAY (EVEN THE TINY ONES 😊)
___
___

WHAT DID I LEARN TODAY?
___
___

GOOD NIGHT THOUGHTS/PRAYERS:
___
___

QUICK DAILY RATING:

😍 EXCEPTIONAL   😁 PRETTY GOOD   😐 AVERAGE   😖 BACK TO THE DRAWING BOARD

The sun is a daily reminder that we too can rise again from the darkness.

TODAY I WILL BE THE SUNSHINE!
DATE:

RELATIONSHIPS I NEED TO CULTIVATE TODAY:

1-

2-

3-

TODAY I AM GRATEFUL FOR:

_____

_____

_____

MY INTENTION & COMMITMENT (ACTION STEPS) FOR THE DAY:

_____

_____

_____

Thoughts/Brilliant Ideas/Musings

REVISIT MY WINS TODAY (EVEN THE TINY ONES 😊)

_____

_____

WHAT DID I LEARN TODAY?

_____

_____

GOOD NIGHT THOUGHTS/PRAYERS:

_____

_____

QUICK DAILY RATING:

😍 EXCEPTIONAL 😁 PRETTY GOOD 😐 AVERAGE 😖 BACK TO THE DRAWING BOARD

Be the sunshine in someone else's day.

Be The Sunshine!

30-DAY REFLECTION

TODAY I AM GRATEFUL FOR: Over the past 30 days—did I see any patterns?

RELATIONSHIPS I NEED TO CULTIVATE: Did I see an improvement in my relationships, and are there relationships I want to cultivate in the next 30 days?

MY INTENTIONS: What did I accomplish in the past 30 days related to my intentions, and are there other areas where I need to focus?

REVISIT MY WINS: Review your wins for the past 30 days! CONGRATS!

DO OVER: What will I do differently in my next 30 days?

QUICK DAILY RATING: What was your average score over the past 30 days—reflect on that rating!

Am I <u>moving closer to</u> or <u>further away from</u> my vision? Check the vision page (page 10).

Gratitude & Reflection turn up the SUN LIGHT!

Be The Sunshine!

TIME TO REORDER YOUR NEXT JOURNAL!

BE THE SUNSHINE JOURNAL MAKES FOR A GREAT GIFT!

Order your journals here and share your experience!

Gratitude & Refelection turn up the SUN LIGHT!

TODAY I WILL BE THE SUNSHINE!
DATE:

RELATIONSHIPS I NEED TO CULTIVATE TODAY:

1-

2-

3-

TODAY I AM GRATEFUL FOR:

_____

_____

_____

MY INTENTION & COMMITMENT (ACTION STEPS) FOR THE DAY:

_____
_____
_____

Thoughts/Brilliant Ideas/Musings

REVISIT MY WINS TODAY (EVEN THE TINY ONES 😊)

_____
_____

WHAT DID I LEARN TODAY?

_____
_____

GOOD NIGHT THOUGHTS/PRAYERS:

_____
_____
_____

QUICK DAILY RATING:

😍 EXCEPTIONAL   😁 PRETTY GOOD   😐 AVERAGE   😖 BACK TO THE DRAWING BOARD

Happiness is found when you stop comparing yourself to other people.

TODAY I WILL BE THE SUNSHINE!
DATE:

RELATIONSHIPS I NEED TO CULTIVATE TODAY:

TODAY I AM GRATEFUL FOR:

1- _____

2- _____

3- _____

MY INTENTION & COMMITMENT (ACTION STEPS) FOR THE DAY:
_____
_____
_____

Thoughts/Brilliant Ideas/Musings

REVISIT MY WINS TODAY (EVEN THE TINY ONES 😊)
_____
_____

WHAT DID I LEARN TODAY?
_____
_____

GOOD NIGHT THOUGHTS/PRAYERS:
_____
_____
_____

QUICK DAILY RATING:

😍 EXCEPTIONAL   😃 PRETTY GOOD   🙂 AVERAGE   😖 BACK TO THE DRAWING BOARD

Smile big, laugh often.

TODAY I WILL BE THE SUNSHINE!
DATE:

**RELATIONSHIPS I
NEED TO CULTIVATE TODAY:**

1-

2-

3-

TODAY I AM GRATEFUL FOR:

_____

_____

_____

MY INTENTION & COMMITMENT (ACTION STEPS) FOR THE DAY:

_____
_____
_____

Thoughts/Brilliant Ideas/Musings

REVISIT MY WINS TODAY (EVEN THE TINY ONES 😊)

_____
_____

WHAT DID I LEARN TODAY?

_____
_____

GOOD NIGHT THOUGHTS/PRAYERS:

_____
_____
_____

QUICK DAILY RATING:
😍 EXCEPTIONAL   😀 PRETTY GOOD   🙂 AVERAGE   😖 BACK TO THE DRAWING BOARD

Sunshine on my mind.

TODAY I WILL BE THE SUNSHINE!
DATE:

**RELATIONSHIPS I
NEED TO CULTIVATE TODAY:**

TODAY I AM GRATEFUL FOR:

1-

2-

3-

MY INTENTION & COMMITMENT (ACTION STEPS) FOR THE DAY:

___

Thoughts/Brilliant Ideas/Musings

REVISIT MY WINS TODAY (EVEN THE TINY ONES 😊)

WHAT DID I LEARN TODAY?

GOOD NIGHT THOUGHTS/PRAYERS:

QUICK DAILY RATING:

 EXCEPTIONAL    PRETTY GOOD    AVERAGE    BACK TO THE DRAWING BOARD

Choose joy, every single day.

TODAY I WILL BE THE SUNSHINE!
DATE:

**RELATIONSHIPS I
NEED TO CULTIVATE TODAY:**

1-

2-

3-

TODAY I AM GRATEFUL FOR:

_____

_____

_____

MY INTENTION & COMMITMENT (ACTION STEPS) FOR THE DAY:

_____
_____
_____

Thoughts/Brilliant Ideas/Musings

REVISIT MY WINS TODAY (EVEN THE TINY ONES 😊)

_____
_____

WHAT DID I LEARN TODAY?

_____
_____

GOOD NIGHT THOUGHTS/PRAYERS:

_____
_____
_____

QUICK DAILY RATING:

😍 EXCEPTIONAL   😄 PRETTY GOOD   😐 AVERAGE   😖 BACK TO THE DRAWING BOARD

The sun never says to the earth, 'You owe me.' Look what happens with a love like that. It lights up the whole sky.

TODAY I WILL BE THE SUNSHINE!
DATE:

RELATIONSHIPS I NEED TO CULTIVATE TODAY:

1-

2-

3-

TODAY I AM GRATEFUL FOR:

_____

_____

_____

MY INTENTION & COMMITMENT (ACTION STEPS) FOR THE DAY:

_____
_____
_____

Thoughts/Brilliant Ideas/Musings

REVISIT MY WINS TODAY (EVEN THE TINY ONES 😊)

_____
_____

WHAT DID I LEARN TODAY?

_____
_____

GOOD NIGHT THOUGHTS/PRAYERS:

_____
_____
_____

QUICK DAILY RATING:

 EXCEPTIONAL    PRETTY GOOD    AVERAGE   😖 BACK TO THE DRAWING BOARD

Happiness is not out there, it's in you.

TODAY I WILL BE THE SUNSHINE!
DATE:

**RELATIONSHIPS I
NEED TO CULTIVATE TODAY:**

TODAY I AM GRATEFUL FOR:

1-

2-

3-

_____

_____

_____

MY INTENTION & COMMITMENT (ACTION STEPS) FOR THE DAY:

_____
_____
_____

Thoughts/Brilliant Ideas/Musings

REVISIT MY WINS TODAY (EVEN THE TINY ONES 😊)

_____
_____

WHAT DID I LEARN TODAY?

_____
_____

GOOD NIGHT THOUGHTS/PRAYERS:

_____
_____
_____

QUICK DAILY RATING:

😍 EXCEPTIONAL   😃 PRETTY GOOD   😐 AVERAGE   😵 BACK TO THE DRAWING BOARD

Sunshine is the best filter.

TODAY I WILL BE THE SUNSHINE!
DATE:

**RELATIONSHIPS I
NEED TO CULTIVATE TODAY:**

TODAY I AM GRATEFUL FOR:

1-

2-

3-

MY INTENTION & COMMITMENT (ACTION STEPS) FOR THE DAY:

Thoughts/Brilliant Ideas/Musings

REVISIT MY WINS TODAY (EVEN THE TINY ONES 😊)

WHAT DID I LEARN TODAY?

GOOD NIGHT THOUGHTS/PRAYERS:

QUICK DAILY RATING:

😍 EXCEPTIONAL   😀 PRETTY GOOD   😐 AVERAGE   😖 BACK TO THE DRAWING BOARD

Laughter is the fireworks of the soul.

TODAY I WILL BE THE SUNSHINE!
DATE:

**RELATIONSHIPS I
NEED TO CULTIVATE TODAY:**

1-

2-

3-

TODAY I AM GRATEFUL FOR:

_____

_____

_____

MY INTENTION & COMMITMENT (ACTION STEPS) FOR THE DAY:

_____

_____

_____

Thoughts/Brilliant Ideas/Musings

REVISIT MY WINS TODAY (EVEN THE TINY ONES 😊)

_____

_____

WHAT DID I LEARN TODAY?

_____

_____

GOOD NIGHT THOUGHTS/PRAYERS:

_____

_____

_____

QUICK DAILY RATING:

😍 EXCEPTIONAL   😄 PRETTY GOOD   😊 AVERAGE   😖 BACK TO THE DRAWING BOARD

A day without laughter is a day wasted.

TODAY I WILL BE THE SUNSHINE!
DATE:

RELATIONSHIPS I NEED TO CULTIVATE TODAY:

TODAY I AM GRATEFUL FOR:

1-

2-

3-

_____

_____

_____

MY INTENTION & COMMITMENT (ACTION STEPS) FOR THE DAY:
_____
_____
_____

Thoughts/Brilliant Ideas/Musings

REVISIT MY WINS TODAY (EVEN THE TINY ONES 😊)
_____
_____

WHAT DID I LEARN TODAY?
_____
_____

GOOD NIGHT THOUGHTS/PRAYERS:
_____
_____
_____

QUICK DAILY RATING:

😍 EXCEPTIONAL   😀 PRETTY GOOD   😐 AVERAGE   😖 BACK TO THE DRAWING BOARD

Stay close to people who feel like sunshine.

TODAY I WILL BE THE SUNSHINE!
DATE:

**RELATIONSHIPS I
NEED TO CULTIVATE TODAY:**

TODAY I AM GRATEFUL FOR:

1-

2-

3-

_____

_____

_____

MY INTENTION & COMMITMENT (ACTION STEPS) FOR THE DAY:

_____

_____

_____

Thoughts/Brilliant Ideas/Musings

REVISIT MY WINS TODAY (EVEN THE TINY ONES 😊)

_____

_____

WHAT DID I LEARN TODAY?

_____

_____

GOOD NIGHT THOUGHTS/PRAYERS:

_____

_____

_____

QUICK DAILY RATING:

😎 EXCEPTIONAL   😃 PRETTY GOOD   🙂 AVERAGE   😖 BACK TO THE DRAWING BOARD

Choose happiness and live life to the fullest.

TODAY I WILL BE THE SUNSHINE!
DATE:

**RELATIONSHIPS I
NEED TO CULTIVATE TODAY:**

TODAY I AM GRATEFUL FOR:

1-

2-

3-

MY INTENTION & COMMITMENT (ACTION STEPS) FOR THE DAY:
_____
_____
_____

Thoughts/Brilliant Ideas/Musings

REVISIT MY WINS TODAY (EVEN THE TINY ONES 😊)
_____
_____

WHAT DID I LEARN TODAY?
_____
_____

GOOD NIGHT THOUGHTS/PRAYERS:
_____
_____
_____

QUICK DAILY RATING:
😍 EXCEPTIONAL   😀 PRETTY GOOD   😐 AVERAGE   😣 BACK TO THE DRAWING BOARD

Let your light shine.

TODAY I WILL BE THE SUNSHINE!
DATE:

**RELATIONSHIPS I
NEED TO CULTIVATE TODAY:**

TODAY I AM GRATEFUL FOR:

1- _____

2- _____

3- _____

MY INTENTION & COMMITMENT (ACTION STEPS) FOR THE DAY:
_____
_____
_____

Thoughts/Brilliant Ideas/Musings

REVISIT MY WINS TODAY (EVEN THE TINY ONES 😊)
_____
_____

WHAT DID I LEARN TODAY?
_____
_____

GOOD NIGHT THOUGHTS/PRAYERS:
_____
_____
_____

QUICK DAILY RATING:

😍 EXCEPTIONAL   😁 PRETTY GOOD   😐 AVERAGE   😖 BACK TO THE DRAWING BOARD

Happiness looks gorgeous on you.

TODAY I WILL BE THE SUNSHINE!
DATE:

RELATIONSHIPS I NEED TO CULTIVATE TODAY:

1-

2-

3-

TODAY I AM GRATEFUL FOR:

_____

_____

_____

MY INTENTION & COMMITMENT (ACTION STEPS) FOR THE DAY:

_____

_____

_____

Thoughts/Brilliant Ideas/Musings

REVISIT MY WINS TODAY (EVEN THE TINY ONES 😊)

_____

_____

WHAT DID I LEARN TODAY?

_____

_____

GOOD NIGHT THOUGHTS/PRAYERS:

_____

_____

_____

QUICK DAILY RATING:

😍 EXCEPTIONAL 😀 PRETTY GOOD  🙂 AVERAGE  😖 BACK TO THE DRAWING BOARD

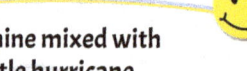

Sunshine mixed with a little hurricane.

TODAY I WILL BE THE SUNSHINE!
DATE:

**RELATIONSHIPS I
NEED TO CULTIVATE TODAY:**

1-

2-

3-

TODAY I AM GRATEFUL FOR:

_____

_____

_____

MY INTENTION & COMMITMENT (ACTION STEPS) FOR THE DAY:

_____
_____
_____

Thoughts/Brilliant Ideas/Musings

REVISIT MY WINS TODAY (EVEN THE TINY ONES 😊)

_____
_____

WHAT DID I LEARN TODAY?

_____
_____

GOOD NIGHT THOUGHTS/PRAYERS:

_____
_____
_____

QUICK DAILY RATING:

😍 EXCEPTIONAL   😀 PRETTY GOOD   😐 AVERAGE   😖 BACK TO THE DRAWING BOARD

Life is better with a little sunshine.

TODAY I WILL BE THE SUNSHINE!
DATE:

**RELATIONSHIPS I
NEED TO CULTIVATE TODAY:**

TODAY I AM GRATEFUL FOR:

1-

2-

3-

_____

_____

_____

MY INTENTION & COMMITMENT (ACTION STEPS) FOR THE DAY:

_____

_____

_____

Thoughts/Brilliant Ideas/Musings

REVISIT MY WINS TODAY (EVEN THE TINY ONES 😊)

_____

_____

WHAT DID I LEARN TODAY?

_____

_____

GOOD NIGHT THOUGHTS/PRAYERS:

_____

_____

_____

QUICK DAILY RATING:

 EXCEPTIONAL    PRETTY GOOD    AVERAGE    BACK TO THE DRAWING BOARD

Happiness is a warm puppy.

TODAY I WILL BE THE SUNSHINE!
DATE:

**RELATIONSHIPS I
NEED TO CULTIVATE TODAY:**

TODAY I AM GRATEFUL FOR:

1-

2-

3-

MY INTENTION & COMMITMENT (ACTION STEPS) FOR THE DAY:
_____
_____
_____

Thoughts/Brilliant Ideas/Musings

REVISIT MY WINS TODAY (EVEN THE TINY ONES 😊)
_____
_____

WHAT DID I LEARN TODAY?
_____
_____

GOOD NIGHT THOUGHTS/PRAYERS:
_____
_____
_____

QUICK DAILY RATING:
😍 EXCEPTIONAL   😄 PRETTY GOOD   😐 AVERAGE   😖 BACK TO THE DRAWING BOARD

A day without laughter is a day wasted.

TODAY I WILL BE THE SUNSHINE!
DATE:

RELATIONSHIPS I NEED TO CULTIVATE TODAY:

1-

2-

3-

TODAY I AM GRATEFUL FOR:

_____

_____

_____

MY INTENTION & COMMITMENT (ACTION STEPS) FOR THE DAY:

_____

_____

_____

Thoughts/Brilliant Ideas/Musings

REVISIT MY WINS TODAY (EVEN THE TINY ONES 😊)

_____

_____

WHAT DID I LEARN TODAY?

_____

_____

GOOD NIGHT THOUGHTS/PRAYERS:

_____

_____

_____

QUICK DAILY RATING:

 EXCEPTIONAL    PRETTY GOOD    AVERAGE   😖 BACK TO THE DRAWING BOARD

Happiness is an inside job.

TODAY I WILL BE THE SUNSHINE!
DATE:

**RELATIONSHIPS I
NEED TO CULTIVATE TODAY:**

TODAY I AM GRATEFUL FOR:

1-

2-

3-

_____

_____

_____

MY INTENTION & COMMITMENT (ACTION STEPS) FOR THE DAY:

_____
_____
_____

Thoughts/Brilliant Ideas/Musings

REVISIT MY WINS TODAY (EVEN THE TINY ONES 😊)
_____
_____

WHAT DID I LEARN TODAY?
_____
_____

GOOD NIGHT THOUGHTS/PRAYERS:
_____
_____
_____

QUICK DAILY RATING:
😍 EXCEPTIONAL   😃 PRETTY GOOD   🙂 AVERAGE   😖 BACK TO THE DRAWING BOARD

You are my sunshine,
my only sunshine.

TODAY I WILL BE THE SUNSHINE!
DATE:

**RELATIONSHIPS I
NEED TO CULTIVATE TODAY:**

1-

2-

3-

TODAY I AM GRATEFUL FOR:

_____

_____

_____

MY INTENTION & COMMITMENT (ACTION STEPS) FOR THE DAY:

_____
_____
_____

Thoughts/Brilliant Ideas/Musings

REVISIT MY WINS TODAY (EVEN THE TINY ONES 😊)

_____
_____

WHAT DID I LEARN TODAY?

_____
_____

GOOD NIGHT THOUGHTS/PRAYERS:

_____
_____
_____

QUICK DAILY RATING:

😍 EXCEPTIONAL   😁 PRETTY GOOD   😐 AVERAGE   😖 BACK TO THE DRAWING BOARD

*Let your joy be in your journey,
not in some distant goal.*

TODAY I WILL BE THE SUNSHINE!
DATE:

RELATIONSHIPS I NEED TO CULTIVATE TODAY:

1-

2-

3-

TODAY I AM GRATEFUL FOR:

___

___

___

MY INTENTION & COMMITMENT (ACTION STEPS) FOR THE DAY:

___

___

___

Thoughts/Brilliant Ideas/Musings

REVISIT MY WINS TODAY (EVEN THE TINY ONES 😊)

___

___

WHAT DID I LEARN TODAY?

___

___

GOOD NIGHT THOUGHTS/PRAYERS:

___

___

QUICK DAILY RATING:

😍 EXCEPTIONAL   😄 PRETTY GOOD   😐 AVERAGE   😖 BACK TO THE DRAWING BOARD

Happiness is a state of mind.

TODAY I WILL BE THE SUNSHINE!
DATE:

RELATIONSHIPS I NEED TO CULTIVATE TODAY:

TODAY I AM GRATEFUL FOR:

1-

2-

3-

_____

_____

_____

MY INTENTION & COMMITMENT (ACTION STEPS) FOR THE DAY:
_____
_____
_____

Thoughts/Brilliant Ideas/Musings

REVISIT MY WINS TODAY (EVEN THE TINY ONES 😊)
_____
_____

WHAT DID I LEARN TODAY?
_____
_____

GOOD NIGHT THOUGHTS/PRAYERS:
_____
_____
_____

QUICK DAILY RATING:

 EXCEPTIONAL    PRETTY GOOD    AVERAGE    BACK TO THE DRAWING BOARD

Sunshine is the best medicine.

TODAY I WILL BE THE SUNSHINE!
DATE:

RELATIONSHIPS I NEED TO CULTIVATE TODAY:

1-

2-

3-

TODAY I AM GRATEFUL FOR:

_____

_____

_____

MY INTENTION & COMMITMENT (ACTION STEPS) FOR THE DAY:

_____
_____
_____

Thoughts/Brilliant Ideas/Musings

REVISIT MY WINS TODAY (EVEN THE TINY ONES 😊)
_____
_____

WHAT DID I LEARN TODAY?
_____
_____

GOOD NIGHT THOUGHTS/PRAYERS:
_____
_____
_____

QUICK DAILY RATING:

😍 EXCEPTIONAL   😃 PRETTY GOOD   😐 AVERAGE   😖 BACK TO THE DRAWING BOARD

Choose joy every day.

TODAY I WILL BE THE SUNSHINE!
DATE:

**RELATIONSHIPS I
NEED TO CULTIVATE TODAY:**

1-

2-

3-

TODAY I AM GRATEFUL FOR:

_____

_____

_____

MY INTENTION & COMMITMENT (ACTION STEPS) FOR THE DAY:

_____
_____
_____

Thoughts/Brilliant Ideas/Musings

REVISIT MY WINS TODAY (EVEN THE TINY ONES 😊)

_____
_____

WHAT DID I LEARN TODAY?

_____
_____

GOOD NIGHT THOUGHTS/PRAYERS:

_____
_____
_____

QUICK DAILY RATING:

😍 EXCEPTIONAL   😁 PRETTY GOOD   😌 AVERAGE   😖 BACK TO THE DRAWING BOARD

Don't let anyone ever dull your sparkle.

TODAY I WILL BE THE SUNSHINE!
DATE:

**RELATIONSHIPS I
NEED TO CULTIVATE TODAY:**

TODAY I AM GRATEFUL FOR:

1-

2-

3-

MY INTENTION & COMMITMENT (ACTION STEPS) FOR THE DAY:
___

Thoughts/Brilliant Ideas/Musings

REVISIT MY WINS TODAY (EVEN THE TINY ONES 😊)
___

WHAT DID I LEARN TODAY?
___

GOOD NIGHT THOUGHTS/PRAYERS:
___

QUICK DAILY RATING:

 EXCEPTIONAL    PRETTY GOOD   AVERAGE    BACK TO THE DRAWING BOARD

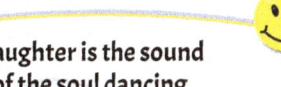

**Laughter is the sound
of the soul dancing.**

TODAY I WILL BE THE SUNSHINE!
DATE:

RELATIONSHIPS I NEED TO CULTIVATE TODAY:

TODAY I AM GRATEFUL FOR:

1-

2-

3-

_____

_____

_____

MY INTENTION & COMMITMENT (ACTION STEPS) FOR THE DAY:
_____
_____
_____

Thoughts/Brilliant Ideas/Musings

REVISIT MY WINS TODAY (EVEN THE TINY ONES 😊)
_____
_____

WHAT DID I LEARN TODAY?
_____
_____

GOOD NIGHT THOUGHTS/PRAYERS:
_____
_____
_____

QUICK DAILY RATING:

😍 EXCEPTIONAL   😃 PRETTY GOOD   😌 AVERAGE   😖 BACK TO THE DRAWING BOARD

You are my sunshine on a cloudy day.

TODAY I WILL BE THE SUNSHINE!
DATE:

RELATIONSHIPS I NEED TO CULTIVATE TODAY:

1-

2-

3-

TODAY I AM GRATEFUL FOR:

___

___

___

MY INTENTION & COMMITMENT (ACTION STEPS) FOR THE DAY:

___
___
___
___

Thoughts/Brilliant Ideas/Musings

REVISIT MY WINS TODAY (EVEN THE TINY ONES 😊)

___
___

WHAT DID I LEARN TODAY?

___
___

GOOD NIGHT THOUGHTS/PRAYERS:

___
___
___

QUICK DAILY RATING:

🤩 EXCEPTIONAL   😃 PRETTY GOOD   🙂 AVERAGE   😖 BACK TO THE DRAWING BOARD

The sun always shines above the clouds.

TODAY I WILL BE THE SUNSHINE!
DATE:

**RELATIONSHIPS I
NEED TO CULTIVATE TODAY:**

1-

2-

3-

TODAY I AM GRATEFUL FOR:

_____

_____

_____

MY INTENTION & COMMITMENT (ACTION STEPS) FOR THE DAY:

_____
_____
_____

Thoughts/Brilliant Ideas/Musings

REVISIT MY WINS TODAY (EVEN THE TINY ONES 😊)
_____
_____

WHAT DID I LEARN TODAY?
_____
_____

GOOD NIGHT THOUGHTS/PRAYERS:
_____
_____
_____

QUICK DAILY RATING:

😍 EXCEPTIONAL   😀 PRETTY GOOD   🙂 AVERAGE   😖 BACK TO THE DRAWING BOARD

Life is better with a little bit of sunshine.

TODAY I WILL BE THE SUNSHINE!
DATE:

**RELATIONSHIPS I
NEED TO CULTIVATE TODAY:**

TODAY I AM GRATEFUL FOR:

1-

2-

3-

_____
_____
_____

MY INTENTION & COMMITMENT (ACTION STEPS) FOR THE DAY:
_____
_____
_____

Thoughts/Brilliant Ideas/Musings

REVISIT MY WINS TODAY (EVEN THE TINY ONES 😊)
_____
_____

WHAT DID I LEARN TODAY?
_____
_____

GOOD NIGHT THOUGHTS/PRAYERS:
_____
_____

QUICK DAILY RATING:

😍 EXCEPTIONAL   😃 PRETTY GOOD   😐 AVERAGE   😖 BACK TO THE DRAWING BOARD

**Happiness is a cup of
tea and a good book.**

TODAY I WILL BE THE SUNSHINE!
DATE:

RELATIONSHIPS I NEED TO CULTIVATE TODAY:

TODAY I AM GRATEFUL FOR:

1-

2-

3-

_____

_____

_____

MY INTENTION & COMMITMENT (ACTION STEPS) FOR THE DAY:

_____

_____

_____

Thoughts/Brilliant Ideas/Musings

REVISIT MY WINS TODAY (EVEN THE TINY ONES 😊)

_____

_____

WHAT DID I LEARN TODAY?

_____

_____

GOOD NIGHT THOUGHTS/PRAYERS:

_____

_____

_____

QUICK DAILY RATING:

 EXCEPTIONAL    PRETTY GOOD    AVERAGE    BACK TO THE DRAWING BOARD

Keep your face always toward the sunshine, and shadows will fall behind you.

Be The Sunshine!

90-DAY REFLECTION

TODAY I AM GRATEFUL FOR: Over the past 90 days—has my gratitude increased/decreased?

RELATIONSHIPS I NEED TO CULTIVATE: Did I see an improvement in my relationships, and which relationships need my focus in the next 90 days?

MY INTENTIONS: What needs my INTENTIONAL focus in the next 90 days?

REVISIT MY WINS: How have your wins over the past 90 days impacted your life?

DO OVER: What will I do differently in my next 90 days?

Time to revisit my vision page (page 10).

Gratitude & Reflection turn up the SUN LIGHT!

About the Author

I created the BE THE SUNSHINE Journal to complement my YOU ARE MY SUNSHINE series of kids books. I believe that each of us has the opportunity to LIGHT UP this world with our unique SMILES.

I am a wife, a mother and am honored to also be an award winning speaker & author. I come from a family based business background and have owned and operated TMC: a national credit card processing company, for over 25 years. My AMAZING team has been recognized for exemplary customer service and for developing and maintaining one of the *Best Workplace Cultures in America*.

As a certified Ziglar Legacy Trainer/Coach, a Master DISC Trainer, certified Business Made Simple Coach and a certified John Maxwell Trainer, I have dedicated my life to improving the lives of the people God places in my path. Attitude & Gratitude have played key roles in that pursuit. This journal is a result of those efforts!

To connect, learn about our training, or place an order, please visit:
www.CheriPerry.com

www.ingramcontent.com/pod-product-compliance
Lightning Source LLC
Chambersburg PA
CBHW042023180426
43199CB00039B/2928